AMERICA'S INDUSTRIAL SOCIETY IN THE 19TH CENTURY ™

Telegraph and Telephone Networks
Groundbreaking Developments in American Communications

Jesse Jarnow

rosen central
Primary Source ™

The Rosen Publishing Group, Inc., New York

Published in 2004 by The Rosen Publishing Group, Inc.
29 East 21st Street, New York, NY 10010

First Edition

Library of Congress Cataloging-in-Publication Data

Jarnow, Jesse
Telegraph and telephone networks: groundbreaking developments in American communications/Jesse Jarnow.
    p. cm.—(America's industrial society in the 19th century)
Includes index.
Summary: This book presents the history of the telephone and telegraph, inventions of the 1800s that gave people new ways to communicate.
ISBN 0-8239-4025-X (library binding)
ISBN 0-8239-4279-1 (paperback)
6-pack ISBN 0-8239-4291-0
1. Telegraph—United States—Juvenile literature 2. Telephone—United States—Juvenile literature
[1. Telecommunication 2. Telephone]
I. Title II. Series
TK5265.J37 2003
621.382—dc21

2003-003673

Manufactured in the United States of America

On the cover: large image: Alexander Graham Bell opening telephone line between New York City and Chicago. First row (from left to right): steamship docked at a landing; Tammany Hall on election night, 1859; map showing U.S. railroad routes in 1883; detail of bank note, 1822, Bank of the Commonwealth of Kentucky; People's Party (Populist) Convention at Columbus, Nebraska, 1890; Republican ticket, 1865. Second row (from left to right): William McKinley gives a campaign speech in 1896; parade banner of the Veterans of the Haymarket Riot; Alexander Graham Bell's sketch of the telephone, c. 1876; public declaration of the government's ability to crush monopolies; city planners' illustration of Stockton, California; railroad construction camp, Nebraska, 1889.

Photo credits: cover, pp. 12, 22 (right) © Bettmann/Corbis; p. 5 © Historical Picture Archive/Corbis; p. 6 © Archivo Iconografico, S.A./Corbis; pp. 8, 10 (right) © The Samuel B. Morse Papers, Library of Congress; p. 10 (left) © National Museum of American History, Smithsonian Institution; pp. 13, 18, 23, 25 © Culver Pictures, Inc.; p. 14 © John M. Read Jr. to Abraham Lincoln, November 7, 1860, available at Abraham Lincoln Papers at the Library of Congress, Manuscript Division; p. 16 © Library of Congress, Geography and Map Division; p. 20 © Library of Congress, Prints and Photographs Division; p. 22 (left) © Alexander Graham Bell Family Papers, Library of Congress, Manuscript Division; p. 26 © Library of Congress, Manuscript Division.

Designer: Tahara Hasan; **Editor:** Jill Jarnow; **Photo Researcher:** Peter Tomlinson

Contents

1
Dashes and Dots

It's easy to talk to a friend who is next to you. But what if your friend is a hundred miles away? Suppose you could shout very loud. It would take over eight minutes for your voice to reach him or her. Sound travels through the air at between twelve and thirteen miles a minute.

In 1791, two French brothers were going to different schools. The schools were close. The brothers could wave to each other in the distance.

The brothers invented a way to send each other messages. They used movable arms on poles. Each position of the arms stood for a letter of the alphabet. It was called the semaphore system. But it worked only on clear days.

In the early 1800s, it took weeks for a letter to travel across the country. A person on horseback could carry it. A horse-drawn wagon could carry it. It could travel on a ship to the port cities of the United States and beyond.

An 1808 illustration of a Royal Mail coach by W. H. Pyne. In 1753, Benjamin Franklin and William Hunter were appointed by the English Parliament as postmasters general for the thirteen colonies. Franklin developed a rate chart for mail that charged according to the weight of the letter and the distance it would travel. This was a major improvement. Franklin was fired by the British in 1774 because he supported American revolutionary activities.

Then steam trains were invented. By 1831, trains in the United States carried mail. Trains were faster than horses. They were faster than boats. Some trains could travel thirty miles an hour! But train tracks didn't run everywhere.

In 1848, mail still traveled slowly. Suppose you wanted to send a letter from New York to California. It traveled from New York to Panama by steamship. The letter crossed Panama by train. The letter was then loaded onto another steamship. It might reach California in a month.

But soon it would be faster to send messages. People had been working on it.

Back in 1752, Ben Franklin had proved that lightning was electricity. He flew a silk kite in a thunderstorm. On the string was an iron key. The string was anchored to the ground with an iron spike. Lightning sent a flash of electricity down the string. It hit the metal key.

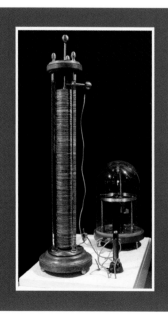

In 1800, Italian inventor Alessandro Volta created his most important invention. He realized that he could make an electric current flow when he connected the ends of a wire to a group of alternating copper and zinc disks that were separated with a cloth soaked in salty water. The first source of continuous electrical current, this discovery led to the creation of the common battery. Shown here is Volta's first non-electrostatic electric generator from 1799.

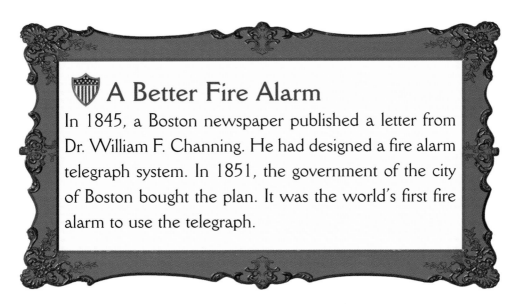

🛡 A Better Fire Alarm

In 1845, a Boston newspaper published a letter from Dr. William F. Channing. He had designed a fire alarm telegraph system. In 1851, the government of the city of Boston bought the plan. It was the world's first fire alarm to use the telegraph.

In 1792, Alessandro Volta built the first electric battery. Volta was an Italian scientist. He used thin sheets of copper and zinc. They were separated with a moist board. Volta made electricity travel across a wire. He showed that electricity could flow like water.

In 1820, Hans Christian Oersted was working in Denmark. He discovered that a wire that was carrying an electric current created a magnetic field. By sending an electric impulse over a wire, you could make a distant magnet move. This is how a telegraph works.

Many inventors came up with ways to send electrical impulses over a telegraph wire and make magnets move to spell out a message. But their inventions were hard to use. Samuel Morse invented a special code. Morse code uses a

> On May 24, 1844, artist and inventor Samuel Morse demonstrated to the public his telegraph equipment and code. He sent a message across a wire from the Supreme Court chamber in Washington, D.C., to his assistant in a railroad depot in Baltimore, Maryland. The tape shown above was inscribed by Morse the day of the demonstration. The letters of the message are written under each letter of the code.

magnetic key that taps out dots and dashes, which stand for letters of the alphabet. It was much easier to learn and use.

In 1844, Morse built a telegraph line. It ran between Baltimore and Washington, D.C. It was forty miles long. Morse telegraphed a message from Washington, D.C., to Baltimore. The message traveled through the wire. It quickly reached Baltimore. It printed out in dots and dashes on a strip of paper.

Morse's message said, "What hath God wrought?" It was a good question. Some people were scared of the telegraph. They thought it was the devil's work. People are sometimes afraid of things they don't understand.

2
Using the Telegraph

Morse code was hard to understand. That's why there were telegraph operators. They read every telegraph message. They had to. Some people didn't like this. They wanted their messages to be private.

Many people invented private codes to use when they sent telegraph messages. Sometimes they changed words around. Sometimes words stood for different things. Sometimes people made up nonsense words. It was very confusing for operators. Telegraph companies tried to stop customers from doing this. But they couldn't.

Telegraph operators made friends with each other. They told stories and traded gossip by telegraph. They played games on the wires. Some people played chess and checkers. Many people never met each other. For them, the telegraph was like the Internet. Telegraph companies couldn't stop this either.

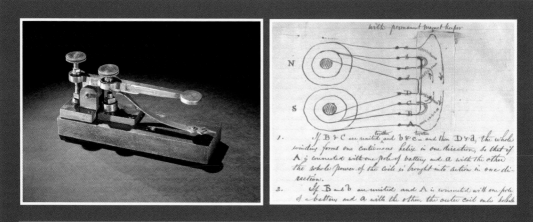

On the left is the telegraph key used by Samuel Morse to send his famous message, "What hath God wrought?" on May 24, 1844. Designed by Morse's assistant, Alfred Vail, this simple strip of spring steel and a metal contact forever changed the world of communications. On the right is a sketch for this invention.

By 1851, Erie Railroad operators knew Morse code. By 1853, the company had set up 497 miles of telegraph line along their tracks. The railroad company built fifty-two telegraph stations. They hired sixty-five telegraph workers.

Many railroads used the telegraph to help improve service. Operators sent messages to stations down the line if a train was running late. They sent special orders to train engineers.

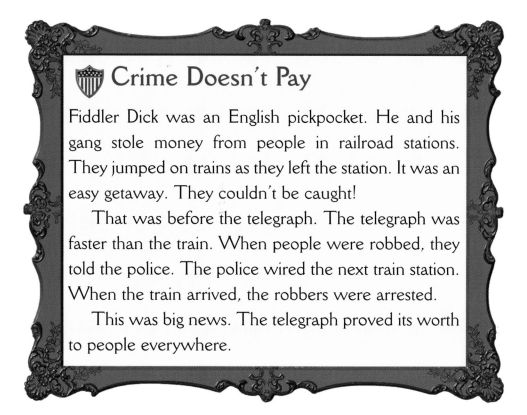

🛡 Crime Doesn't Pay

Fiddler Dick was an English pickpocket. He and his gang stole money from people in railroad stations. They jumped on trains as they left the station. It was an easy getaway. They couldn't be caught!

That was before the telegraph. The telegraph was faster than the train. When people were robbed, they told the police. The police wired the next train station. When the train arrived, the robbers were arrested.

This was big news. The telegraph proved its worth to people everywhere.

By 1861, over 50,000 miles of telegraph lines covered the United States. There were 2,250 telegraph offices in the country. People sent huge numbers of telegrams.

But telegrams were expensive. Only rich people and businesses could afford them. Companies sent telegrams about business deals. They wanted their money to grow faster.

To send a telegram, a person went to a telegraph office. An operator tapped out the message on a keypad. The

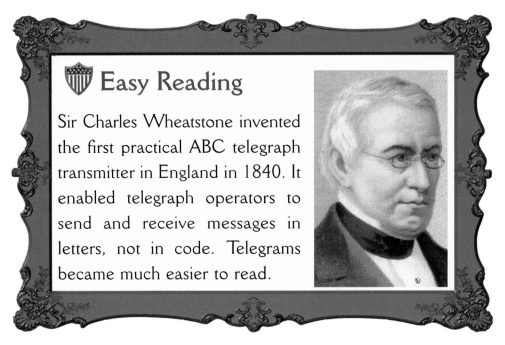

Easy Reading

Sir Charles Wheatstone invented the first practical ABC telegraph transmitter in England in 1840. It enabled telegraph operators to send and receive messages in letters, not in code. Telegrams became much easier to read.

message traveled across a long wire. An operator at the other end received it. The message was given to a messenger who delivered it.

Every city in America had a telegraph office. They were busy places. Some telegraph offices were huge. They had many floors. Some had nearly five hundred telegraph machines. People carried messages from one part of the office to the other. Offices had rooms for newspaper reporters. They had dining rooms for workers. Some even had doctors' offices!

The telegraph was an important tool in the American Civil War (1861–1865). Each army had its own code.

A 600-person switchboard in the main operating room of Western Union in New York in about 1889. The arches above the operators are pneumatic tubes that carried printed messages quickly to and from city stations by using the force of air pressure. Pneumatic tubes are still used today by some banks and hospitals.

They planned battles. They asked for supplies. Sometimes the armies of the North and South read each other's secret messages. When they could, they cut down each other's telegraph lines.

There was no telegraph office at the White House. So President Abraham Lincoln visited the War Department's

On November 7, 1860, John M. Read Jr. sent this telegram from Albany, New York, to Abraham Lincoln in Illinois to congratulate him on his triumphant presidential election.

telegraph office every day. He read the messages that had arrived from Union army leaders. He learned about victories and defeats. The messages helped him make important decisions.

3

From Sea to Shining Sea

In 1862, President Lincoln signed an important act. It called for the building of train tracks across the country. It would be the transcontinental railroad. The North and the South were fighting the Civil War, so the tracks were built across the North, far from the battlefields.

The Central Pacific Railroad began to lay tracks in Sacramento, California. They would travel east. The Union Pacific Railroad began laying tracks in Omaha, Nebraska. They would travel west. The tracks would join in Utah.

The Union Pacific Railroad hired many Irish immigrants. They laid tracks for hundreds of miles. Their route was mostly through plains. They toiled in hot and cold weather.

The Central Pacific Railroad had to lay tracks through huge mountains. They didn't have enough reliable workers. So they hired 12,000 immigrants from China. These

This 1883 map of the United States was created by Rand, McNally & Company for a report on internal commerce for the United States Bureau of Statistics. Highlighting the Pacific railroad lines, this map also shows details of drainage, sloping land, international and state boundaries, cities, towns, forts, roads, and other parts of the railroad network.

people worked very hard. The Chinese labored for twelve hours each day. They worked six days a week. At the most, they earned $35 a month.

The work was very dangerous. The Chinese workers chipped roadbeds through the rocks. They were lowered

over cliffs in baskets. They hammered at rock walls and inserted dynamite. The weather was terrible. There were many accidents. More than a thousand Chinese workers died.

Building the transcontinental railroad was a race. People followed it in newspapers. By 1869, the race was almost over. The two railroads would soon meet.

On May 10, 1869, the train tracks joined in Utah. There was a big ceremony. People drank champagne and gave speeches. A band played.

A telegraph wire had been installed at the site. An operator watched the celebration. He telegraphed the news

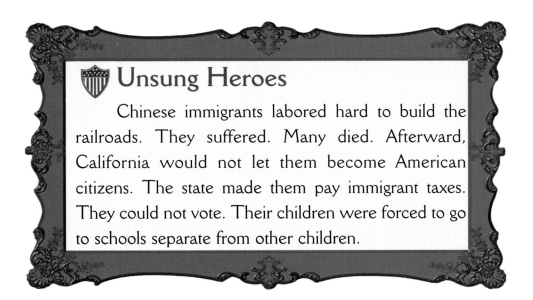

Unsung Heroes

Chinese immigrants labored hard to build the railroads. They suffered. Many died. Afterward, California would not let them become American citizens. The state made them pay immigrant taxes. They could not vote. Their children were forced to go to schools separate from other children.

across the country. A person could now cross the country by train. It would take only ten days! This was big news.

The operator had tied a telegraph wire to the last spike. The sound of the spike being hammered would travel through the wire.

On May 10, 1869, in Promontory Point, Utah, chief engineers Samuel S. Montague (Central Pacific Railroad) and Grenville M. Dodge (Union Pacific Railroad) shook hands to celebrate the completion of the first transcontinental railroad. The rails of the UPRR reached westward from Omaha, Nebraska, to join with those of the CPRR, which reached eastward from Sacramento, California. To announce the coast-to-coast connection, a telegraph operator sent out a simple message to the nation: "DONE!"

The owners of the railroad companies were there. Their jobs were to hammer in the last spike. It was gold. They both drank too much champagne at the ceremony. They swung their hammers. But they both missed!

Next, people wanted to send telegrams across the ocean. In 1857, Cyrus W. Field and Frederick Gisborne began to place a telegraph line at the bottom of the Atlantic Ocean.

Underwater Messages

It's 1867 in New York City. A machine clicks in a telegraph office. Dots and dashes appear on a long strip of paper. A man picks up the paper. He reads the code. The message was tapped into a wire in London. From there, the signal ran through wires lying at the bottom of the Atlantic Ocean.

The message traveled thousands of miles through the ocean. It came up in Nova Scotia. From there, it traveled by wire down the Atlantic coast. It took over sixteen hours for the message to reach its destination. Many people thought it was magic.

In 1855, it took a week or more for a message to travel to the United States from Europe. Canadian Frederick Gisborne and New Yorker Cyrus W. Field *(seen at left)* dreamed of changing this. Creating a company to lay the first telegraph cable across the ocean, they struggled against the elements, nearly succeeding many times. In the end, the cable always snapped. In 1866, a sturdy cable was finally in place, ushering in the information highway.

The wires would be very long. The job was difficult. The wires snapped many times. In 1858, Europe and the United States were finally connected. But the cable snapped after three weeks. It took until 1866 for it to work properly.

Telegraphs became very popular. The wires were very busy. Sometimes it was hard to get messages through. People wanted to solve this problem. They wanted to send many messages at the same time. They wanted messages to travel faster.

4
Nothing But a Toy

One person working to make the telegraph faster was Alexander Graham Bell. He invented the harmonic telegraph. It used tuning forks to turn Morse code into sounds. His assistant was Thomas Watson. They lived in Boston.

In 1875, they made an important discovery. It was an accident. Watson was tuning the telegraph. The sound went through the wire. Bell could hear it in the next room! This gave them the idea for the telephone.

In March 1876, their telephone worked for the first time. Again, it was because of an accident. They were experimenting with batteries. Bell spilled sulfuric acid on himself. "Mr. Watson, come here, I want you!" he said. Watson was in the next room. He heard Bell over the wire!

Bell and Watson exhibited their invention. Bell brought the telephone to large halls. Watson stayed behind at the

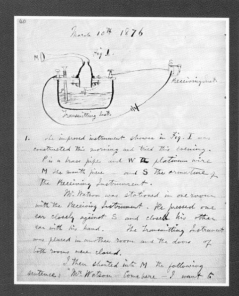

On the left is a sketch from the notebook of Alexander Graham Bell from March 10, 1876, in which he describes the day he called to his assistant, Thomas A. Watson. His voice traveled through his experimental equipment and was heard in the next room. On the right is an early Bell telephonic device that he used to give demonstrations in June 1876.

lab. Bell would call Watson on the phone. Watson sang into his end of the telephone. Sometimes he played records. Watson's voice came out of the mysterious box. People listened. They marveled at the invention.

The sound was still weak. So Watson had to sing very loud. The neighbors were very annoyed.

Watson bought some hoops for holding together wooden barrels. He connected them and put a blanket

These wooden phones were available in New York City at J. H. Bunnell & Company in the late 1800s. The phones shown here had circular mouthpieces built into the main body and separate earpieces from which to hear. Replacement receivers and transmitters, pictured at the bottom of the page, were available. To make a call with one of these phones, a person spoke to an operator in a main office who connected one phone to another.

over them. He stood inside with the phone and sang. The blanket kept the sound from bothering the neighbors. It was the first telephone booth.

In 1876, Bell offered to sell his invention to the Telegraph Company for $100,000. This was the age of big business in America. Yet business magnates could not see the value of Bell's invention. The Telegraph Company appointed a group to study the offer. The group wrote a report. They called Bell's telephone a toy. They did not buy it. Big mistake!

5

The Bells Are Ringing

Bell could not sell his invention. So he opened his own company. It was called the Bell Telephone Company. Bell and his father-in-law, Gardiner Greene Hubbard, ran it. Hubbard was a major investor in the company. Soon, there were telephones in over 3,000 houses. The next year, 10,000 phones were in service.

Other people tried to start telephone companies, too. Bell had a big battle with the Western Union Company. It bought the rights to a telephone from another inventor. But Bell had the first patent.

There were many lawsuits. Bell's company won them all. The other companies had to close.

Bell's patents lasted until the middle of the 1890s. Until then, Bell controlled all the telephone service and the equipment in the country.

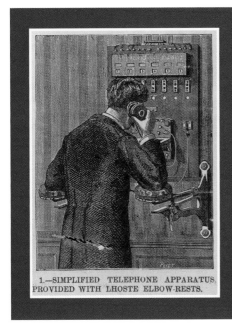

1.—SIMPLIFIED TELEPHONE APPARATUS PROVIDED WITH LHOSTE ELBOW-RESTS.

This telephone from 1884 includes armrests to ease the caller's long wait for information or for resting during long conversations. Early telephones ran on batteries. Once a month, a worker changed the batteries that ran the microphone. Batteries that ran the transmitter and the bell were replaced about every four months.

The equipment was the telephone. The company owned people's phones. They leased them. This meant that people paid to rent them. If a phone broke, the company fixed it.

The service was the network. A phone is good only if there are other phones to call. The Bell Telephone Company connected phones to each other.

Making a call was harder than it is today. A person picked up the telephone and turned a crank. This sent a signal to an operator in an office. The operator worked at a switchboard. The operator asked the customer whom he or she wanted to call. The operator rang the telephone of the other person. If someone answered, the operator connected the wires.

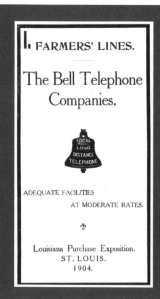

FARMERS' LINES.

The Bell Telephone
Companies.

ADEQUATE FACILITIES
AT MODERATE RATES.

Louisiana Purchase Exposition.
ST. LOUIS.
1904.

In 1894, Bell's second telephone patent ran out. Until then, only the Bell Telephone Company was licensed to operate telephone systems in the United States. By 1904, however, over 6,000 independent telephone companies had opened. But these new companies were not interconnected. People using small companies could not reach each other by telephone. In this 1904 brochure, Bell Telephone advertises to farmers, explaining how telephones will benefit them and their businesses.

Operators knew the names of all the customers. In 1897, there was a measles epidemic. A doctor in Massachusetts worried that many operators were out sick. The new operators did not know the customers' names. How could they connect anyone? So each phone was given a number. When a person picked up the phone, an operator would say, "Number, please."

Sometimes it was hard to hear on the telephone. There was often a lot of noise. Sometimes it took a long time to get connected. The Bell Telephone Company worked to fix the problems. They put in new wires. They designed new switchboards. They created new methods. They searched for ways to make phone service better.

Bell's patents ran out in 1894. Soon many other telephone companies opened. There was a lot of competition. As a result, the price of telephones went down. Most of the other companies weren't as good as Bell's. But they provided telephone service in new places. More people could have telephones.

The telegraph had made it possible for people to send messages faster than ever before. But to send a telegraph, a person had to go to an office. Telephones changed the country, yet again.

More people got telephones. Telephones became cheaper. The way people used telephones changed, too. They weren't just for business. People used telephones at home. They could call across the street. They could call across town. Some people could call across the country.

In 1880, there were 50,000 telephones in the United States. By 1890, there were 250,000 telephones. By 1900, 800,000 people had telephones!

The telegraph and the telephone were very important inventions of the 1800s. They gave people new ways to communicate. They changed people's sense of time and distance. They made the world seem smaller. Things happened more quickly. These inventions challenged people to think about the world in new ways.

Glossary

harmonic telegraph (**har-MAH-nik TEH-lih-graf**) A kind of telegraph that could send more than one message through the same wire. Alexander Graham Bell was working on the harmonic telegraph when he discovered that voices could travel through a wire.

lease (**LEES**) To pay a fee to use somebody else's property.

magnetic field (**mag-NEH-tik FEELD**) The area around a magnet where its force of attraction is felt.

magnetism (**MAG-nuh-tih-zum**) The force that pulls certain objects toward a magnet.

Morse code (**MORS COHD**) A language of dots and dashes invented by Samuel Morse for use on the telegraph.

network (**NET-werk**) A group of people or things that are interconnected.

operator (**AH-puh-ray-ter**) A person who works the machinery associated with the telephone, the telegraph, or other machines or devices.

patent (**PA-tint**) A document that stops people from copying an invention.

switchboard (**SWITCH-bord**)   A system of wires used by operators to connect telephone lines to each other.

telegraph (**TEH-lih-graf**)   A machine used to send messages through coded electric signals over wires.

telephone (**TEH-lih-fohn**)   A communication device that allows users to speak to each other by sending their voices through wires.

toil (**TOYL**)   To labor; to strain.

transcontinental (**tranz-kon-tin-EN-tul**)   Going across a continent.

Web Sites

Due to the changing nature of Internet links, the Rosen Publishing Group, Inc., has developed an online list of Web sites related to the subject of this book. This site is updated regularly. Please use this link to access the list:

http://www.rosenlinks.com/aistc/tetn

Primary Source Image List

Page 5: Drawing of Royal Mail coach by W. H. Pyne, 1808. Historical Picture Archive/Corbis.

Page 6: Electric generator by Alessandro Volta, 1799. Archivo Iconografico, S.A./Corbis.

Page 8: First telegraph message, May 24, 1844. Samuel Morse Papers, Library of Congress.

Page 10: At left, Samuel Morse telegraph key used May 24, 1844. On public display NMAH, Smithsonian Institution. At right, a drawing by Samuel Morse, Samuel Morse Papers, Library of Congress.

Page 12: Portrait of Sir Charles Wheatstone (1802–1875). Bettmann/Corbis.

Page 13: Engraving showing main operating room of Western Union, New York. *The Telegraph of Today*, circa 1889. Culver Pictures.

Page 14: Telegram from John M. Read Jr. to Abraham Lincoln, delivered by the Illinois & Mississippi Telegraph Company on November 7, 1860. From the Abraham Lincoln Papers, Library of Congress.

Page 16: Map published by Rand, McNally & Company, Chicago, for the United States Department of Commerce and Labor, Bureau of Statistics, 1883. Library of Congress.

Page 18: Photograph of joining the rails, Promontory Point, Utah, May 10, 1869. From the Seidman Collection. Culver Pictures.

Page 20: Photograph of Cyrus W. Field, half-plate daguerreotype, gold-toned, produced by the studio of Matthew Brady sometime between 1844 and 1869. Daguerreotype Collection, Library of Congress.

Page 22: At left, notebook entry by Alexander Graham Bell on March 10, 1876, Alexander Graham Bell Family Papers, Library of Congress. At right, early Bell telephonic device, June 1876. Corbis.

Page 23: Catalog page from J. H. Bunnell & Company, New York City. Artwork signed W. J. Howell, circa late 1800s. Culver Pictures.

Page 25: Engraving by Poye, circa 1884. Culver Pictures.

Page 26: Bell Telephone Companies advertising pamphlet produced for use at the Louisiana Purchase Exposition, St. Louis, Missouri, 1904. From the Alexander Graham Bell Family Papers, Library of Congress.

Index

About the Author

Jesse Jarnow is a Brooklyn-based writer and editor. He writes mostly about loud music and big explosions. His work has appeared in *Signal to Noise*, *Relix Magazine*, *11211*, *Hear/Say*, and the *Anonymous Church of the Hypocritical Prophet*. He is a graduate of the Oberlin College creative writing department and a former member of the Studio 77 Art Collective.